FROM VICTIM TO SURVIVOR

Gillian Jackson

Raider Publishing International

New York   London   Cape Town

© 2011 Gillian Jackson

All rights reserved. No part of this book may be reproduced stored in a retrieval system or transmitted in any form by any means without the prior written permission of the publisher, except by a reviewer who may quote brief passages in a review to be printed in a newspaper, magazine or journal.

First Printing

The views, content and descriptions in this book do not represent the views of Raider Publishing International. Some of the content may be offensive to some readers and they are to be advised. Objections to the content in this book should be directed towards the author and owner of the intellectual property rights as registered with their local government.

All characters portrayed in this book are fictitious and any resemblance to persons living or dead is purely coincidental.

Cover Images Courtesy of iStockPhoto.com

ISBN: 978-1-61667-376-5

Published By Raider Publishing International
www.RaiderPublishing.com
New York London Cape Town
Printed in the United States of America and the United Kingdom

Introduction

In the past five years my life has been completely turned around. After over forty years of silence, I finally admitted that I had been sexually abused as a child. I cannot say that I've had a terrible life because of my past but it has always been there, a secret festering inside and preventing me from living as my real self. It's difficult to describe; it's almost as if I have only ever been a cardboard cut-out of what I might have been and now, at the age of fifty-four, I'm at last developing into a rounded, filled out person.

My experiences over the last few years have prompted me to write this book in an effort to help others who have carried similar terrible secrets and are now crumbling under the weight. It's the book I would have wished to read at the start of my journey. There are several excellent books on the subject of healing from childhood abuse but I personally found them too complex. I needed something simple and straightforward, encouraging and not patronizing. I don't think I even had the energy to lift those weighty books when I was at my worst, nor plough through psychological theories I'd previously never heard of. Yes, I've read some of these amazing books since but they were just not appropriate for me at the time.

The purpose of this book is to be an aid to understanding the impact of childhood sexual abuse on victims. Many adults go through life with traumatic memories from their infancy, which they try to hide, not just from others, but also from themselves. These memories may stay hidden for many years but the reality of what happened in childhood can affect the way we live in the present. It can prevent us from being 'complete' adults, from forming healthy relationships, and from the happiness and contentment that could be ours.

To gain a sense of freedom from our past, it is necessary to deal with the issues and put them into context. If you have been sexually abused in the past, it is a fact that cannot be changed. Ignoring it, hiding it in some deep recess of your mind, or pretending it didn't happen will not work. Yes, these pretences can appear to work and many victims have led fulfilled and reasonably happy lives, keeping the secret for many years. But to all victims, the past is never completely hidden. There will be triggers which cause painful memories, news items which have similarities to your own experience, places, people and even certain smells can take you back to that place you don't want to be in. Surely it's far better and healthier to confront your memories and work through them and then it will be the appropriate time to file them away under 'sorted'.

The gender terms in this book are generally female, perhaps because I am, but it is intended for both male and female readers. It is also for people of any sexual orientation or age, although parental or adult supervision would be appropriate for younger teens and children.

It is not my intention to add to the growing list of 'misery memoirs' that appear on bookshop and supermarket shelves but rather create something much more practical than just sharing an experience

FROM VICTIM TO SURVIVOR

Gillian Jackson

1

Using This Book

Any book can of course be read from cover to cover but this one is designed to be read with more flexibility. We are all different and what suits one, does not always suit another. Some chapters stand alone, like Chapter Five on counselling. This can be used as a reference and to see which options are available. Other chapters, like Chapter Six, Coping with Emotions, can be dipped into at any time you feel the need. Obviously the final two chapters are probably best read in sequence but if you are anything like me, you will want to flick through it all to see what you're getting.

Chapter Two is my own story. It is written to let you know where I am coming from and is in no way graphic. The book can be used without reading this chapter but I hope my experiences, in this and other parts of the book, will serve to encourage you along the way. We all doubt our sanity and 'normality' at times, so hopefully you will be encouraged to know you are not alone in some of your darkest moments and weirdest thoughts.

If you are at the point where you have someone you trust who is helping you along the way, you may wish to share this book with her. Working together with a 'buddy' gives an alternative perspective to some points and will help your friend or partner to understand what you are going through. Discussion of certain issues can help clarify what is the best route for you.

I have tried to include practical ideas of things which may aid recovery. Yes, these things take time and effort, which are often both in short supply but the benefits of making the effort can be worth it and the rule is to begin slowly and build up.

If the copy you are reading is your own copy, feel free to make notes in it. Perhaps something you wish to explore further will crop up and you can mark it for future reference. You may wish to jot down your thoughts and reactions to certain points. This can be helpful but if your writing is of a confidential nature, keep your book in a secure place.

Don't read anything you are not comfortable with, you can leave it until later when you feel ready to go down that path, or you can just skip it all together. This book is designed to help you in the healing process; if it isn't helping then perhaps you're not ready yet.

At the end of the book are helpline and web site contact details. There is a lot of help out there; you need never struggle on your own. Healing of childhood traumas is a process. We are never completely free from the effects and even if it has been several years since you tackled the issue, there may be times in your life when you need a little extra support. These organizations are specifically formed for this. They are staffed with dedicated and caring people, many of whom have been prompted into this kind of work by their own experiences. They are on your side. Don't hesitate to ask for help when you are struggling, we all need support sometimes.

2
Author's Story

The complexities of keeping secrets can be a heavy weight to carry around. The burden grows heavier with passing time and, like telling lies, compounds as the secrets age.

I used to be scornful of women who claimed to be depressed. In fact I didn't believe in depression, adopting a 'pull yourself together' attitude, which in hindsight, shames me. I prided myself on being one of life's 'copers,' conforming to the image I wanted to create: a devoted wife, a good mother, a competent homemaker and hostess and a generous contributor to local community activities. My life was busy and for the most part fulfilling but there was always a sense that I was acting out this role. Was I pretending to be what I thought I should be? Was I trying to live the life others had come to expect of me? I don't honestly know but the years brought happiness in my family life and success in business as I pioneered Day Nurseries in my hometown, opening and managing the first one in the town in 1987.

Today I wonder if my choice of career has been shaped by my early experiences in life. I had always had a concern for young children and for as long as I can remember wanted to teach but circumstances led me into training for pre-school care and education and I always loved my work.

I also acknowledge that I was an over protective mother. Not to the point of being suffocating but I trusted no one to care for my own children as well as I could. Fortunately they have grown into happy, well-adjusted adults of whom I am extremely proud.

So why did I crack after forty years of secrecy and silence? With hindsight I can identify a number of incidents that were perhaps triggers, bringing old memories to the fore. As the manager of a fifty place, day nursery, it was inevitable that at some point I would encounter instances of abuse. Generally I could be objective and professional in such cases and I worked with the support of an excellent staff and the social services department. In the later years of my work in the nursery we cared for a little girl, not then two years old, who we discovered presented physical signs of sexual abuse. It was an upsetting case and I floundered a little in my responsibilities, passing this case to my deputy. In fact this was the correct thing to do. My deputy was the most amazing, caring person I knew who already had a rapport with the child concerned and her mother. For me, this was perhaps the first trigger, the first time I had to acknowledge to myself that I had buried the traumas of my own childhood deep inside, trying to hide them from myself as well as my world.

Shortly after this incident, my health began to fail me. A long term back problem was degenerating and osteoporosis developed. This necessitated selling the nursery after thirteen years of building it up and living and working on the premises. It was to be a huge change in lifestyle and in many ways the loss of my identity. This loss was similar to that of bereavement and I was beginning to show signs in my mental health that all was not well.

Another significant contribution to my eventual breakdown was a new role in life as a grandmother. This seems such a contradiction as becoming a grandmother is one of life's best experiences. I found it every bit as emotional as becoming a mother had been twenty-eight years previously. All my maternal feelings were again brought to the fore, coupled with that overwhelming protective instinct that almost knocks you off your feet. It was a wonderful time in many respects. I had the privilege of attending my grandson's birth, amazing! But I felt lost, scared and fearful for the future.

I eventually had to concede to the fact that I was depressed and the 'pull yourself together' school of thought failed me. My family had noticed and although I fought it, trying to push my rising emotions back inside myself, I could no longer function normally. It seemed that I spent the best part of a year in tears without really being able to explain why.

I am fortunate in having an extremely caring husband who has played an enormous part in helping me overcome my negative childhood memories. He is the one in whom I first confided. In fact he actually guessed what was troubling me after seeing my distress and listening to the snippets of the nightmares I shared with him. He is the one who persuaded me to seek help from my general practitioner (GP), which was, for me, the start of my road to confronting my past and moving on with my future.

Initially I found it enough to admit to my doctor that I was unable to cope and after asking various questions, he declared me to be clinically depressed, prescribed a form of Prozac and arranged blood tests to check hormone levels. This seemed logical and I went along with his suggestions while all the time I was guiltily aware that I was only telling him half the story. During a later visit, when the blood tests had come back as normal, my doctor gently lectured me about patients who expect their doctor to do his job with only half the tools he needs. I knew exactly what he meant. GP's see many patients who present a medical problem, while in reality wanting another problem solved. We expect our doctors to be mind readers and I actually thought mine was when he talked to me about things from the past that eventually catch up with us. He painted a word picture of windows of opportunities in life which out of the blue seem to present us with the opportunity to deal with past traumas. We can use these windows of opportunity or not; I decided to use this one. Forty years of hiding, even from myself is a long time and I had had enough.

As a little girl, I was sexually abused by an 'uncle' over three or four years. This abuse began when I was four years old.

There. I have typed the words. They are set out in black and white and it's never easy. I do not intend to go into details about the abuse; this book is about you, not me. I have no desire to write a 'misery memoir' as it seems fashionable to do. The purpose of my declaration is to help you realise you are not alone; that you can deal with this, and that it isn't, and never was, your fault. There is life after abuse! I may refer to my own experiences at times in this book to illustrate certain points and to hopefully encourage you in your own recovery.

When I began to trust my doctor and be completely honest with him, he could begin to help me tackle my problems. The prescriptions continued, I felt better for taking the tablets and symptoms such as panic attacks and flashbacks were lessened with the medication. Professional counselling was the next step. Letters were written, appointments made and assessments attended until I was finally introduced to a specialist counsellor who began to work with me. That all sounds remarkably simple but it isn't. There are waiting lists, it isn't instantaneous, but it's worth hanging in. The counsellor felt I would benefit from attending group sessions. Shock! Horror!

It had taken me forty years to get to this point; did she know what she was asking? Did she not understand how difficult it had been to tell my husband, my doctor? And now she wanted me to become part of a group? My initial reaction was to say a resounding no! Fortunately there was yet another waiting list and my name was added, without having to make a definite commitment, and by the time the group met, I had been persuaded. I was at the point where I was ready to try anything and I am so grateful I did. This weekly group session, which I attended with such trepidation, proved to be one of the most powerful experiences of my life. I shall expand on this in Chapter Five when we can look at the counselling options in greater detail. For the moment I will simple say don't rule anything out. When you make this decision to confront your past, look at all the options and help available so you can make an informed choice on which route is the best for you. That is not to say don't listen to professional advice, I would have never progressed if I hadn't taken advice and trusted people along the way, but you don't have to do anything that you really don't want to. This whole process is for your wellbeing, to support you in your journey to move on and be happy.

It is also important to remember that it will take time and effort. Don't expect the professionals to do all the work; they won't. They'll help and guide, make suggestions, support and listen to you. You will have to take responsibility for your own healing but it's worth it, you're worth it. Be prepared to live with a stranger – you. For at least two years I didn't know who I was. My attitudes had changed; my behaviour was erratic to say the least. I don't know how my husband stuck with me but I'm so glad he did. Looking back, I think I was perhaps back in some missed stage of my childhood, pushing boundaries and testing those who loved me as a child does with her parents. I had been too afraid to do that as a child, so perhaps I was revisiting a childhood stage which I needed to go through.

This journey is an education. I know and understand myself much better now than I have ever done. I don't like everything I've found out about myself, but I have a greater understanding about why I am how I am and why I do what I do. In short, I'm more at ease with myself than I have ever been, which is what I wish for you.

3
Telling Someone

If you are reading this book by recommendation of a counsellor, the chances are that you have already shared your experiences with a professional and are on the way to getting help. If you have told no one, then perhaps this could be your window of opportunity.

I cannot stress strongly enough that you were then a child, a different creature to what you are today.

Firstly, let's look at the reasons why victims of childhood abuse don't tell. It is vitally important to always remember that you were a child when this happened. You were an innocent, you needed to be loved and protected because you were too young to do that for yourself. Your vocabulary was that of a child, your thoughts were those of a child and your actions were those of a child. When you remember the abuse now, you are remembering it with adult eyes. Your actions, thoughts and powers of expression are now those of an adult. I cannot stress strongly enough that you were then a child, a different creature to what you are today. If you have trouble remembering what it was like to be a child, find a photograph of yourself from those days. Keep it close by as you read this book; it could be your bookmark. Look at that child. Would you expect her to have the same knowledge and wisdom you have today? Would you expect her to look after herself and stay safe? Would you expect her to articulate her thoughts and feelings, to be able to explain what she doesn't understand herself? That child was you; you didn't understand what was happening to you and you didn't realise it was wrong. You didn't have the words to express what was physically happening, never mind to stick up for yourself or tell a trusted adult. And didn't you trust all adults? Your expectation was that the adult cared for you and did what was best for you, that should have been your right but the reality was quite different.

"If you tell..."

But perhaps there are more sinister reasons why you didn't tell. Abusers know what they are doing, they make plans, they 'groom' their targets. They create opportunities and use persuasion, bribes and threats. Maybe it was a 'special secret' just for the two of you, which made you feel important. It could have been the presents you were given, again designed to make you feel special, and we all want to feel that we matter. Or it could have been the threats. Threats are usually designed to frighten a child into silence and can be quite complicated.
"If you tell, no one will believe you and they'll hate you for telling lies."
"If you tell, you'll be taken away from home."
"If you tell, I'll kill you and Mummy and Daddy."
Can you see how these threats are designed to put the responsibility for what is happening on the child? Children generally believe what adults tell them; it's in their nature to trust. This all sinks into a child's mind until they believe that what is happening is actually their fault.

Look at your photo again. Could that child really be responsible for a paedophile's actions? Absolutely not! You were targeted and manipulated and worst of all is that most victims still believe, well into adulthood, that they were to some degree responsible. If it sounds ridiculous to you, that's great, you're not carrying all that guilt, but if you have been a victim then you can probably understand those feelings of guilt. They have been very real to me at times.

So why don't we tell when we are older and understand that the abuse was wrong? Again that guilt is a big part of the answer to this. When something has been a secret for a long time, it's difficult to bring it into the daylight. We are almost brainwashed into sharing the guilt, it becomes our 'dirty little secret' when in fact it is the abuser's 'dirty little secret.' The child is never to blame.

Apart from the guilt feelings, there is the shame. Again this is another form of guilt. Why should we be ashamed? You were the innocent victim; the shame is all the abuser's.

Another big question is "Will I be believed?" If you

were told as a child that no one would believe you, then you probably still think this as an adult. Yes, we all want to be believed and obviously it helps if we have someone who can corroborate what we say. An abuser may have targeted more than one sibling or another family member may have been aware of your plight. It's not easy to approach someone you may feel knows what happened and obviously much depends on your relationship with them but the help and support you need, a possible 'buddy,' could be on your doorstep. Strangely in my own experience, it didn't occur to me that I wouldn't be believed, except perhaps from one family member. When I did speak out, my sister had known all along and had actually tried to tell our mother at the time. She was, however, a child herself and unable to make herself understood. We had never talked about it, she, because she thought I had forgotten the incidents she had witnessed, and I, because I thought she may have suffered in the same way and I didn't want to stir memories for her.

Obviously it will be hard if you are not believed by family and friends and it may cause divisions but you will be believed by the professionals who are there to help you overcome your problems. Your health and wellbeing is their priority. It may be upsetting for family members to know the truth but it is the way for you to find healing from your past.

You have the right and the ability to make your own decisions.

Telling the authorities is another block that prevents some victims from opening up. They think they will be pressured by family, friends and medical professionals to report the incidents to the police. This decision is yours alone. Certainly the medical services you may turn to will not exert any pressure to do so. Perhaps this is a reason to choose carefully which family members or friends you do tell; it must be someone you trust completely, who will support what you want to do in regard to reporting. The time has already lapsed; historic abuse is different to rape as medical evidence does not come into play, there will be no DNA samples to collect. I personally feel that the best reason to report it to the police is if you think your abuser could still be targeting children. This brings a sense of urgency into the equation and I'm sure that no victim would want to see history repeating itself with another child. In such cases, the police will be very sensitive and discreet. Their main concern will be to stop further offences; they will not put pressure on you to pursue your own case unless you wish to do so.

There will probably come a time when you do want to report it to the police. If your abuser is still alive, in my case he wasn't, seeing him living his life without being accountable for what he has done is hard to bear. He is the perpetrator, yet you are the one who suffers. Many victims have found it liberating to begin the legal process and eventually see some degree of justice. You may want to pursue this course one day but initially you are the priority, what you want and need is the main issue here. Your recovery from your childhood trauma is a process, a journey. You will almost certainly go through peaks and troughs; your emotions will be unfathomable and hard to understand. Each day will bring up different feelings and you will hardly know yourself.

When you do confide your past to someone with the intention of seeking help, the relief is enormous. The years of carrying this alone are over. You have begun the journey.

4
Starting the Journey

If having told someone is beginning the journey, then you are on the way to recovery. Unfortunately there is no map to plan your route, you are going to places you have never been before but you don't have to travel alone. There is help available from many sources and you can choose your companions. It's your journey and you are at the wheel, even if you need help in hanging onto it at times. The journey is entirely for your benefit.

There is no time scale for this journey either. Recovery is a process and each individual is different and will move at her own pace. Do not pressure yourself to complete the journey in a certain amount of time. You may find you need breaks, occasionally or regularly. If you have carried your experiences for many years, healing is going to take time and patience. Don't set yourself any goals at the beginning. This may be helpful as you continue but only small achievable goals. For example, if getting dressed in the morning is a problem to you, make that your goal. Don't be hard on yourself.

Having to deal with anger is part of the process but it must be tailored to an acceptable way. We won't all get it out of our system in the same way.

The process for each individual is different, but experiences are often similar. For example, you may have to deal with issues of anger. This is a natural, even expected emotion for victims but we don't all express anger in the same way. I have seen women shout and swear, I have learned words I didn't know existed and they found relief in that. Great. But what about the quiet woman who never swears and can't find an outlet for her anger with which she is comfortable. She may have religious convictions and expressing anger in such a brash and vocal way would compound her sense of guilt. Having to deal with anger is part of the process but it must be tailored to an acceptable way. We won't all get it out of our system in the same way.

You also need to be ready to move on in your own time, again something which will vary as much as human nature does. You don't have to take any action that you are not comfortable with, perhaps a suggestion may not be right for you, or might not be right for you at that particular time. Be ready for each stage as you tackle it, don't rush yourself.

There seem to be many 'don'ts' coming out here but there are plenty of 'do's' as well. Doing things involves work and you may not always feel like work. I have emphasized not to rush or do anything you are not ready for but the exception to this would be in keeping appointments. At times this will be hard work but the benefits make it worth the effort. I started the process rather reluctantly, particularly the group sessions, but they very quickly became a life-line and I lived for Wednesday afternoons when I could attend this group.

On a more practical side, do keep track of your journey. It may take time to find out how best to do this but it will be a tool for you to chart your progress and an encouragement to look back and realise what you have accomplished. Journals are the most obvious way of doing this, either a weekly or daily account. Note form would be fine or reams of prose, if you are so inclined. If you are into technology and rarely separated from your laptop, you may wish to use this means of recording your journey. Do remember to keep anything you wish to remain private in a safe place. If you really don't get on with the written word, perhaps you could be more practical. Drawing and painting are good mediums for expressing feelings. You don't have to be an artist to do this, shapes, colours, doodles and squiggles can be sufficient, perhaps with titles or words of explanation. We will look at other ideas in more detail in Chapter Seven, but if you make some attempt to record your thoughts and feelings from the beginning, you will be encouraged through the later stages.

You have the ability and the right to be in control of your own life.

Doing something practical, and using our hands, has an added benefit of taking control of our actions. As an abused child, you had no control over the situation and those feelings may continue into adult life. This journey is about healing and taking back control. You have the ability and the right to be in control of your own life.

5
Counselling

It is probable that some crisis in your life brought you to the point of disclosure, telling someone. Your greatest need now is to get rid of the pain and begin the healing process. I found that one of the most powerful aids in my own journey was an understanding of where I was at, and why and how I got there. This process is an education. You will learn about yourself and your relationships, and you could be in for a few surprises. Hopefully you will also learn that you are not alone in what you have experienced and in your healing process. Most importantly, you will learn to understand that what happened to you was not your fault.

Knowing a little of how children develop emotionally and psychologically can help us to understand ourselves today. If we look for a little while at how a child develops and the greatest influences on that development, we can build a base to help our own 'wounded child' to recover.

If you have heard of only one psychologist then it will most likely be Sigmund Freud. He is generally thought to be the founder of psychodynamic counselling. His theories of child development, and what happens in later life if this development is hampered, have revolutionized thinking since the early 20th century. Other theorists have built on these ideas and developed their own, so consequently today, we have a wide base of information and insight into the workings of the human mind. One of Freud's associates, Carl Jung, called the child 'the wonder child.' He identified stages in a child's development, which provide the building blocks for adult life. If we have been wounded in childhood, our development has been arrested, and our trust has been broken, This will very often affect stages in later life. Look at your photograph again and think about what a child is meant to be. The wonder child is naturally optimistic, he is naïve, trusting and vulnerable. Each child is unique, resilient and open. He is curious which leads to exploration and learning. A child needs to be and feel safe, to know that he matters and that his parents are there for him. Children have magical thinking; their world is egocentric, (it revolves around themselves). They believe that if they want something to happen strongly enough then it will. "If I kiss a frog it will turn into a prince."

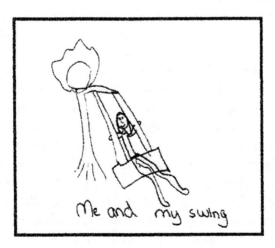

Repression changes these traits. A child's vulnerability leaves him open to abuse and a whole new scenario begins when the child must adapt to get his needs met. His behaviour may present problems, he could be withdrawn and he could learn over time to manipulate as he has been manipulated. Not that he will turn into an abuser, although tragically this can happen, but he has to adapt to get his basic needs met. The instinct for survival can change the course of his or her life. In adulthood, the shame and guilt of what happened to you as a child brings pain. It makes you feel hopeless and life can seem unbearable. Often we take it out on others or cover it up with addictions, not necessarily drugs, but overeating, smoking and drinking. The magical beliefs that are part of growing up can continue and contaminate adult thinking:

"If I had more money, things would be fine."

"If I could get a husband, my life would be better."

"If I prove myself academically, everyone will like me." and so it goes on.

A child with no strong sense of his own values may grow up continually trying to please others. He may have no sense of who he really is, and therefore difficulties in forming and keeping relationships.

The wounded child has no sense of his core self. We are made up of layers, like an onion. These layers are the values we acquire as we grow. Ideally we should develop our own values and be true to our core, our real self. In reality, many of our values come from outside influences, what psychologists' term introjected values. Many of these are positive influences, a parent teaches what is good and what is bad in society. When these influences are negative or where trust has been broken, as in the case of the abused child, everything is distorted A child with no strong sense of his own values may grow up continually trying to please others. It can be like losing a sense of trust in and connection with his true self. He may have no sense of who he really is and therefore have difficulties in forming and keeping relationships which meet his deeper emotional needs.

So what has all this to do with counselling? Counsellors are trained to understand how the mind works; they will give time and space for you to tell your story and work through the different and sometimes difficult emotions that you may be experiencing. They will work to empathise (understand how things feel for you) with your experiences and emotions. Their aim is to help you become a fully functioning adult, able to make your own decisions and shape your own life. As I mentioned before there are different theories of counselling and specialist counselling. They are completely non-judgmental, unshockable (yes, they really have heard it all before) and most importantly on your side. They will not bully you, or persuade you into any course of action you are not comfortable with. They will listen and reflect what they hear. They may offer advice, explain things to you and generally be there for you. Your counsellor will explain clauses of confidentiality too. What you tell her will go no further, with few exceptions such as if you are planning to commit a crime or hurt a child. Counsellors who are members of a regulating body such as the British Association of Counselling and Psychotherapy (BACP) are bound to work in a way which meets professional and ethical standards of care. Counselling is a relationship and the majority of clients find this unique relationship a turning point in their lives.

Counselling will give you a structure to help you on your journey.

The starting point for referral is generally your GP. Now we all know how busy doctors are and you may feel that he has no time to listen to your problems. Yes, appointment times are usually restricted to ten or less minutes but you can book a double time appointment to discuss available options. That sounds so easy doesn't it? But it might not be and you may feel embarrassed or nervous about telling your doctor your problems. Of course, you don't have to go into all the details with him. He will be happy to refer you for a counselling assessment. This is an appointment with a counsellor, who will assess your needs and decide which type of counselling would be best for you. You can always ask questions and have your say at any point in the process. You are dealing with professional, compassionate people whose vocation in life is to help you and others like you.

As with all national health referrals, this is a process and will take time. There are of course private counsellors and if you are in a position to use this facility then again your GP can advise you on who is practicing in your area.

The time factor has it's positives as well as its negatives. The obvious negative is having to wait when you really needed help yesterday. Your doctor may be able to help with interim medication, which thankfully these days is not addictive if used with medical supervision. There are also many organisations who can offer immediate emotional support, if not counselling. These include rape and sexual abuse centres which vary in each area and national organisations such as Victim Support. It doesn't matter that the crime is historic or that it was not reported to the police. Victim Support provides excellent emotional support and anyone can self-refer. If there is not a branch near you, contact the nearest branch, they will have people working in your area. The positive aspect of waiting is that it will give you time to prepare yourself. If you are waiting for group therapy to begin, you will have the chance to arrange time off work or solve other practical problems. You will also be able to prepare mentally by reading a book like this one or finding a local support group. Waiting times vary in different areas, as do venues. Many hospitals have women's centres, where specialist counselling takes place. Some GP surgeries have rooms designated for counsellors to use. Generally these counsellors come in from other areas, a good way to ensure confidentiality. For teenagers, many schools have a counselling service available but I would still recommend that you start with your family doctor. Schools counselling services are excellent but in cases of childhood abuse specialist counselling is advisable.

Counselling is also available through sources other than the National Health Service. Most areas have centres for rape and abuse counselling and include childhood abuse in their remit. Local options can be found in the phone book or on the net and I have listed some national organisations at the end of this book.

Counselling will give you a structure to help you on your journey. You will find help and support, be able to have questions answered, and be sympathetically monitored throughout the process.

In chapter two, I referred to group sessions. My counsellor specialized in psychosexual problems, in particular historic cases of child abuse. I had begun a relationship of trust with her but the mention of group sessions struck horror into my very being. She didn't push me into attending but explained the group dynamics and told me how others had been helped through attending. The group was what she called a 'survivor's group,' a gathering of women with similar experiences. I was assured that I could attend as a spectator with no pressure to contribute to discussions. In my mind I had a vision of some sort of AA meeting where we all had to introduce ourselves and admit that we had been abused in childhood. How very different it actually was. The first week I was silent, although very emotional. A verbal contract was formed to ensure confidentiality and respect for each other. We were a group of strangers, different backgrounds, ages and experiences but by the end of our twelve weeks together we had bonded, finding strength in each other, support and encouragement, and yes, at times we laughed and cried together. I had always feared that there may be someone attending who I would know and that was indeed the case. I was embarrassed, and so was she, but we quickly became firm friends and are still in contact today.

We met for two hours each week for twelve weeks. The first two or three times, it was an effort for me to go but as we began to bond I started to look forward to these sessions. It was an education, sometimes not very pleasant, as we covered such topics as why abusers abuse but it taught me much about myself, gave me a feeling of not being alone in what I had experienced and helped me put my past into perspective. The very name, 'survivor's group' gave us all a sense of power. We adopted a much more positive mindset and stopped thinking of ourselves as victims.

This group was all female but there are male equivalent sessions, which are just as much in demand. If it is hard for women to disclose, then I am sure it is even harder for men. They have the added burden of a macho image to contend with. A boy will feel that he could have done more to stop his abuse than a girl and may possibly find it harder to admit that he was a victim of such.

During the twelve weeks I attended, the survivor's group became the most important date in my diary. I discovered that I was not alone, that I wasn't going mad, I was in fact quite normal in my reactions, and most importantly, it was not and never had been my fault. This was probably the turning point for me, when I began to feel stronger and more empowered. Yes, I could face up to my life, but not only that, I could enjoy it, something I had forgotten how to do.

    Above all, I took away from these sessions the truth that it is not what happened in your past that defines who you are, but rather how you deal with it and move on into the rest of your life.

6

Coping with Emotions

We have already touched on some of the emotions this journey of healing will bring. From the time you first tell someone, disclose, you will most probably have encountered a whirlpool of emotions in which you feel you may drown. The reason for this is that disclosure brings memories and emotions to the fore, which you have suppressed or denied to yourself for months or years. This is natural, it doesn't mean you are going mad (although at times you may feel that you are) and you are perfectly normal in experiencing such emotions, intense though they may be.

You will probably feel that you are experiencing the whole spectrum of human emotions from one extreme to the other and often in such a short space of time, if not simultaneously. Keep hanging on to the fact that this is normal and is part of the process. You will eventually come through it.

Recognising an emotion such as anger is the first step to dealing with it.

Unfortunately, the emotions you experience are generally negative, from anger to hatred, low self-esteem and guilt, as well as many more which unless dealt with can become destructive.

Anger is perhaps the overriding emotion for many. We feel angry with our abuser, angry with those who should have protected us, and angry with ourselves. You may even direct this anger to those closest to you who are completely blameless.

Recognising an emotion such as anger is the first step to dealing with it. Expressing anger needs to be thought out and controlled. Planning to be angry may seem rather strange but it does help to get this emotion out into the open. In Chapter Four, we looked at how dealing with anger needs to be done in a way to suit the individual. Some people may feel the benefit of having a good shout and scream, punching pillows or hammering on the wall; others would feel silly doing such things and may find it helpful to channel their anger into something constructive, aerobic sport or heavy gardening perhaps. Whichever way suits you, it is important to do it in a safe environment where you will be alone, or possibly with your buddy, and your actions will not affect others, particularly any children in the house. It was suggested to me, as a person who rarely expresses anger that I drive out into open countryside and scream as loudly as I could. I did try this and felt some release, but it wasn't really for me, and I probably scared a few sheep too. I found a method of expressing anger that had the benefit of giving me a well-pruned garden one summer. With pruning shears in my hands, I felt I could express my anger and be in control, letting my imagination run riot and laughing out loud as I snipped away.

But there are many more emotions than anger. We can feel a depth of sadness that we have never experienced before. Our self-confidence is at a low ebb and feelings of guilt, shame and self-loathing are common. Of course there are medical aids for such feelings of depression and we may find that we need this extra help at such a difficult time. Naturally these should only be taken under medical supervision. Your GP knows your medical history and should be able to offer advice on the most suitable medication for you. Anti-depressants are much improved to what they were years ago and can be used temporarily without addictive side effects.

It may help to look at the emotions you are experiencing as part of the process of healing. Understanding the stages we go through helps us to cope better and avoid some of the feelings of utter hopelessness and despair that accompany negative emotions.

Whatever brought you to the point of disclosure, whether a full-blown crisis or just some small trigger, was the beginning of these healing stages. You have broken your silence and the most important thing to do now is to get rid of the pain that you have been carrying around for too long. These are some of the stages you can expect:

Understanding that what happened to you was most certainly not your fault. I seem to keep repeating this but I feel it is so important to realise that you were not in any way to blame and should not harbour such thoughts, even in the deepest recesses of your mind.

Acknowledging your hurt and pain. You have already begun this by your disclosure. You have admitted what happened to you, which is never easy, and now you are working to move on with your life. Do you know how brilliant it is that you have got so far? It's an amazing step you have taken and you should be proud of your courage. Acknowledging what happened also helps you put it where it belongs, it is history. It happened, you can never change that, but you can get over it and enjoy the rest of your life.

The angry stage will probably be an on-going emotion which will surface at times when you least expect it. Try to manage your anger by such means as suggested above but if it is really a problem, your GP can arrange professional anger management therapy. Your anger is, to a point, justifiable but there does come a time when hanging on to that anger is only harmful to yourself. With help and time you will be able to let go of this destructive emotion and when you do, it will most likely bring a sense of relief and release.

Sorrow is also part of the healing stage. Of course you will feel sorrow. You have lost your childhood, the innocence and joy which growing up should have given you. It is comparable to bereavement and therefore will obviously take time. Allow yourself this time to grieve. Look at your childhood photographs and remember the little child you were.

Coping with this sorrow is part of the healing process. We all cope in different ways, and so there can be no time scale. No two experiences will be the same, so it follows that no two recovery times will be the same. We all have setbacks that interrupt the process. Life will not go on hold until we are ready to resume living, so we will have the highs and lows of everyday life to contend with. Remember that setbacks can be overcome. The rule is not to set unrealistic targets and time scales; give yourself the time you need.

I include forgiveness here as one of the stages of healing but I do so knowing full well that it is probably the hardest thing of all to do and I would stress that this a very personal thing and certainly not a necessary requirement to complete healing. I include it because I have known it to be a sticking point for many victims on the road to becoming survivors. Some have stumbled here because of religious beliefs. They may have been told at some point that they must forgive their abuser in order to be completely healed. For some this may be the case. It is my opinion that it's not worth the effort of trying your hardest to forgive if you cannot naturally do so. I suppose what I'm trying to say is don't get hung up about it. Don't let this be your sticking point. It's natural to feel emotions as strong as hatred for your abuser but eventually this will be a self-destructive emotion. Many people find that pursuing justice through the courts is the best way to go. Justice is far more satisfying than revenge and hatred and has the constructive effect of stopping your abuser from targeting other children. Naturally each case is different and your counsellor should be able to help you decide which is the best course of action in your circumstances. Forgiveness and legal recompense are things that can be considered at a later date, for the time being, you are the important one and your healing is the priority. In my own case, my abuser had been dead a long time before I disclosed. If he had not been, then I have no doubt that after the help I had received I would have been strong enough to pursue a court case. As things are I feel that perhaps acceptance rather than forgiveness is what I personally have found.

Another part of the healing stage is learning to love yourself. I have mentioned such emotions as self-loathing and low self-esteem. It's natural that your confidence will have been shattered and you may have trouble even liking yourself, never mind loving yourself. Things we have done in the past may make us squirm with guilt and shame but again the key word here is 'past.' Your childhood, or lack of it, may have something to do with the decisions you have made in life. If you are to move on, it will be by forgiving yourself for past mistakes and learning from them. Don't dwell on things you regret. It is well documented that childhood abuse lowers our self-esteem and makes us feel unworthy of the best things in life.

Relationships may be affected by our own low opinions of ourselves, indeed almost everything we do is affected by the way we see ourselves. Learning to love yourself is important.

In the next chapter we look at some ways of giving ourselves time, time to get to know and love ourselves and time to understand who we are.

7
Self Help

In chapter six we looked at some of the stages that happen along our journey; stages that will bring such a variety of emotions that we will, at times, be totally confused. We have looked at the way our attitudes and understanding can help us to cope but what about more tangible ideas. It is medically recognised that being active is good for our minds as well as our bodies, so how can we help ourselves in a practical way? In treating depression doctors may recommend exercise of some form, even if it's only walking the dog. Physical activity produces endorphins, chemicals, which are the body's natural anti-depressant and pain relief; therefore activity helps. Keeping our minds and hands active is also good for us in other ways; we have less time to think of our problems and dwell on the past and are less likely to fall into the trap of feeling sorry for ourselves. Now, doesn't all that sound simple? No, I haven't forgotten about motivation and I know you probably have very little of that at this time. Getting up in the morning is often a major effort so perhaps going to a gym or out jogging is impossible at the moment. How about a ten minute walk? It's better than nothing.

A healthy balanced diet is not only good for our bodies but also our mind and mood. Yes, this takes time and effort but the benefits are worth it. Comfort eating, over eating and junk food is all very tempting but it affects the way we feel, makes us lethargic and generally unwell. Choosing the healthy option will make a big difference to your energy levels and when you are struggling with life, every ounce of energy is precious.

Perhaps a more creative approach will help. Again the rule must be to find something that interests you personally. It's no good taking up landscape painting if you hate the outdoors and can't stand the smell of paint. Start with something simple. If you enjoy writing, then a daily diary or journal could be ideal. This can be a very personal log of your journey, which you can personalise with drawings, photographs, or even by just decorating the cover. An alternative to this would be a scrapbook. The advantage of having things written down is that you can look back and see how far you have come and what you have achieved, a great encouragement when you feel down.

If you don't want to write in depth, a simple feelings chart could help. You could write down just one or two words about how you're feeling each day, which again provides a record of your progress. Another possibility is a 'mood box.' This is quite simply a box in which to keep items that make you feel positive about yourself. Things you might like to included are:

> Photographs of yourself as a child, a special event or family gathering.
> A soft toy.
> Something tactile, perhaps in your favourite colour.
> A book you enjoyed or a magazine.
> A favourite CD or DVD.
> A scented candle.
> Scented bath oil.
> A letter or greeting card that has special meaning.
> Favourite chocolate bar.

Do you see the pattern? It's all about you. A mood box, or bag if you prefer, can be used to cheer you up when you feel down. It can be used to treat yourself to that soak in the bath, or listen to some uplifting music. Half an hour with a magazine can be a treat but go easy on the chocolate! Using a tool like this is giving yourself the gift of time, confirming that you are worthy of such, which is tremendously important.

Some of what I'm suggesting may sound childish but that's the point! You have missed out on a chunk of your childhood and perhaps need to experience some of those things that you missed. Why should teddy bears be only for children? I have several soft toys that I have used for comfort when I've needed to. A teddy is very good at keeping secrets and he's not shocked at what you confide about your innermost feelings. To go even further down that road, I recently experienced the comforting sense of crawling into an improvised 'house' between two pieces of furniture under a blanket. Cushions and a radiator made this a cosy and warm place to be. I was actually sharing it with my two year old granddaughter but I sensed a feeling of peace and safety and could happily have spent time in there alone with a good book. Why not? Finding a safe place for yourself is important. It could be in your own home, or a favourite coffee shop, or even the library; somewhere you are comfortable and relaxed.

> *Your heart pounds and you can't breathe, you might feel sick or dizzy and you think you're having a heart attack, or at the very least going to faint.*

The above suggestions are in a way planned self-help but what about those times when we are taken by surprise such as a panic attack. These can happen at any time and in any place. Your heart pounds and you can't breathe, you might feel sick or dizzy and you think you're having a heart attack or at the very least going to faint. If you are aware of panic attacks and understand what is happening to you, they are much easier to control. Breathe deeply from the abdomen and try to focus your mind on something other than how you are feeling. Do something repetitive, like counting, or if possible occupy yourself with something physical, like making a coffee or knitting. Panic attacks are brought about by memories, often triggered by the most unlikely event. Tell yourself that you are an adult now and in a safe environment. These memories are of the past; keep focused on the present. Some people have found it useful to learn some basic relaxation techniques, such as yoga exercises, which they can draw upon when a panic attack occurs.

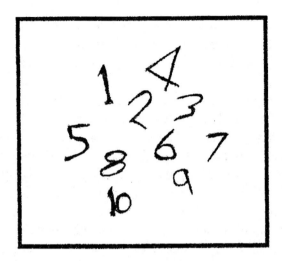

Sleeping can often be a problem for those coping with trauma. Obviously there will be help available from your GP but first you might like to try some of the relaxation and pampering techniques suggested in this chapter. Those of you who are parents know the value of a good routine for babies and young children at night. A winding down with bath time and stories settles children better than rough and tumble play, getting them over excited. So as adults we should try similar strategies; reading, music or whatever relaxes you, followed by a warm bath with a few drops of lavender oil may help. Although no more than six drops or it could have the opposite effect. A cool bedroom is better than a hot one for inducing sleep and avoiding stimulants such as tea and coffee could also help.

The possibility of sharing your journey with a 'buddy' may not be for everyone. Some people are very private and it may be enough to share with the professionals who are helping you but if you do find it helpful to talk and have a close relationship with a friend, partner or sibling, then you could set up a buddy relationship with them. I would suggest that you allot a specific time for this, perhaps a weekly coffee hour. If you spend every moment of your time with this buddy discussing your problems, you may find it difficult to return to your previous friendship when that time comes. Maintaining the relationship as it has always been is healthy and using the buddy side of the friendship for an interim period only while you need extra help is the way to ensure things will return to normal.

Making time to pamper yourself, exercise, write or share with a buddy are all important but you must also allow yourself time to feel sad and grieve. You have experienced the loss of a big chunk of your childhood and it is the same as any major loss, you will need time to reflect. No time scale can be set for this, we all process thoughts and emotions differently; therefore for some the grieving will be over quickly, yet others will find it a slow process. The practical self-help you give yourself will provide tools to understanding yourself and by charting your progress you may find patterns, which will help you to know what triggers your moods and memories.

Finally, at the beginning of this chapter I mentioned walking the dog. I am a great believer in animals for therapy. Naturally you have to be an animal lover for this to work for you. I have found immense comfort in my two cats and in other pets I've owned over the years. Dog owners will know how faithful dogs can be. We can be blessed by owning a pet, enjoying its company and having a focus other than ourselves. They provide entertainment, company, affection, a reason to get out and about, and are loving and giving in return. Ideally, pets and their care should be available on the national health. This is not going to happen and I know that caring for a pet is impossible for many for practical and financial reasons. It may be however that you can have the benefits of a pet without the responsibilities. There are elderly people with pets who cannot exercise them and may be glad of the offer of help. Animal shelters are always seeking volunteers to help with all aspects of care, so you see you can have the best of both worlds if you feel you would benefit from a pet.

Wow, reading back through this chapter seems as if I've presented you with a mountain to climb. Use these ideas in a 'pick and mix' way; you'll be exhausted if you try to introduce everything immediately. Choose what appeals to you and add to the list as you move on.

Self-help is rather like a snowball; you start it rolling and it will run away with you. Your ideas will keep growing until soon you may even find yourself writing a book to encourage others!

8

Relationships

Human beings are not meant to be solitary creatures. Some of life's most satisfying experiences are found in our contacts with others, whether they be family, friends or partners. Building and maintaining good relationships is learnt during childhood. Children have a natural curiosity about other children and an open and trusting faith that all relationships they experience will be good. When this trust is broken, as in the case of childhood abuse, the pattern for building solid, healthy relationships is soured. A child will be confused about who can and cannot be trusted, who is showing genuine love and who is displaying self-gratification at the child's expense. If the child's relationship with an adult is not constant and positive, that child will be unable to learn how to form constant, positive relationships in adult life.

Your abuse was not, in any way, of your own making!

In the case of sexual abuse in children, there is the added confusion about sexuality; what is normal, healthy and acceptable. The child will see sexual relationships as being one sided, unpleasant and even violent. Obviously this will cause problems in adult life. Many victims experience great difficulties in maintaining a sexual relationship. I have known some who find the very thought of a physical relationship abhorrent and for them, completely out of the question. Thankfully this does not have to be the case. Although we all have the right to choose to live in whichever state we find most comfortable, regarding relationships.

As with most of this journey, understanding how and why you feel as you do is the first step. I hope by now that you will have accepted that your abuse was not, in any way, of your own making. I keep going back to that point as I feel it is pivotal to recovery; it certainly has been for me.

If your childhood has been tainted by this abuse, you will most likely have problems with trust in relationships. It will be difficult for you to trust a partner but also yourself. There may be times when you have a very real fear of abandonment (low self esteem feeds this one) and times when you fear engulfment and perhaps just want to avoid human contact. It is difficult to give of yourself in a relationship when you are unsure of who you are and what you want. The wounded child inside the adult has little sense of his authentic self and confusion occurs. We confuse dependency with love and we may have very little experience of what love really is.

The more you begin to understand yourself and the effect which childhood abuse has had upon you, the more you will understand your relationship problems. As each individual's experiences are so different, there are no set rules to help. Hang on to the fact that you can change the way you are living if you wish to. As you grow in self-confidence, you will learn your own needs and how to make relationships work for you. There is of course specialist help available in this area and many women I have known have gone on to make use of such help. Again the rule is not to put pressure on yourself. Work at your own pace and move on only when you feel ready.

    Communication is of paramount importance in any relationship and as you continue your journey it is likely that you will feel more comfortable in expressing your feelings. Some people find that disclosure is like a dam bursting and they begin to talk and can't stop. You may need to go through this phase but choose whom you talk to carefully. Partners and close family can find your journey emotional for themselves and to constantly be going over the same ground may open up wounds for them or pressurise them into feelings of guilt. Use your counsellor for this kind of intensive talking or perhaps a support group or telephone help-line.

You will one day be able to look back on your experiences and realise they have made you a stronger person.

    Moving on to family relationships, these can be just as complicated as partnerships. It is likely that the abuser will have been a family member or close family friend. When your abuse becomes known, the whole family can be devastated. Family splits occur, with members taking sides. This is tragic but all too common. A mother may refuse to believe that her husband or brother could have done such a thing. A sibling may accuse you of lying because their experience was vastly different. In all cases you are expected to act like a diplomat at a time when you are least able to do so. For your own sake, avoid getting into family arguments. This is so hard to do but your own wellbeing is the important factor in all of this and you cannot move on if you are embroiled in constant family disputes. It may not be easy but try to distance yourself in such situations. If a family member refuses to believe you, then that is their problem; you have enough of your own. Your revelations will be a shock to your family and reactions are bound to be varied.

In cases where you feel someone has known but they deny it, do try to give them the benefit of any doubt. You may not feel they deserve this but it is in your own interests not to get into arguments and hold resentments. These will help no one. You will only become frustrated and perhaps bitter at a time when you need to focus on getting well and keeping calm.

If you feel that it would be inappropriate to tell some family members of your experience, then that's fine, an elderly grandparent for example. It's your decision and for whatever reason if you feel that's best, then that's okay. You are not obliged to tell anyone.

In Chapter Six I mentioned forgiveness. This is a problem for some people, not just in regard to their abuser but also members of their family who they feel should have been there for them. If you can talk this through as a family, that's great but dwelling on what should or should not have happened won't help in the long run. What happened to you cannot be changed and other people's part in it cannot either. There may be regrets but heaping feelings of guilt on others will not help you to move on. As for your abuser, the best way to deal with him or her is through the justice system but only when you are ready.

Moving through this healing journey will change you and your relationships. New relationships can be enriched rather than marred by what has happened to you. By this I mean that what you have learned can make you a more compassionate person. Your experiences, although undoubtedly bad, can give you an empathy with others that can give a depth to relationships and friendships now and in the future. This book is all about changing negatives into positives. You will one day be able to look back on your experiences and realise they have made you a stronger person.

9

The Onward Journey

I want to finish this little book by telling you what a wonderful person you are! Yes I am completely serious. Each human being is unique. We all have qualities and depths that are individual to us alone. If you are reading this book and have suffered some kind of sexual abuse during your formative years then that is tragic. It should not have happened but it did. You are still, however, unique and special, perhaps even more so than if you had not experienced such adversity.

This book is about turning negatives into positives, becoming survivors, not victims. You are already on the way to doing that. You can be proud of your achievements so far, even if reading this is your first step. Attitude is all important in this journey. You will find it so much easier with a positive mindset. You are going to get over this and lead a happy and fulfilling life. Keep telling yourself this!

Always be the optimist; look for the sun after the rain.

What happened to you can never be changed but it is history and it can be put into perspective like all historical facts can. You will always have memories and there will be times when these memories will be triggered, possibly by the most unlikely and unexpected things. With time and help, you will be able to 'box' these memories and keep them where they belong, in the past.

You will always have the option of asking for help. I have included a list of help lines and web sites at the end of this book to give you some idea of the support that is out there for you to access. To find more local addresses, you can visit these web sites to get the appropriate help you need. We all flag at times and there's no shame in asking for help that is the purpose of these organisations.

There are traps to avoid as you progress in your recovery. I have suggested earlier that it is helpful to set small achievable goals, which can be useful, but now I would warn about having expectations about how you should be feeling. Notice that word 'should.' The phrase 'tyranny of the shoulds' is an excellent phrase to help us realise that 'should' can be a tyrant! If you are constantly thinking that you 'should' be feeling better or be further along the road, stop and ask yourself who says I should? Remember there is no timescale to your recovery; you can take all the time you need. I think the word 'ought' is also a tyrant, so for the future don't be ruled by 'should' and 'ought.' Just as in the past, you cannot dwell on 'what if' and 'if only.' These words are a waste of your time and a drain on your energy.

I have talked about loving yourself earlier in this book but I want to finish with it now. You can learn to love yourself, even if there are things you don't like about yourself. You can learn to have confidence too. There are techniques to learning how to be confident, even classes to attend. Loving yourself doesn't mean preening in front of a mirror or admiring your physical attributes; it's more about looking deep inside to find your hidden depths, to find the compassion and love that is in you. You were born as an innocent baby and what you missed out on in childhood can be made up for now. Love yourself and you will learn to love life. Become a 'glass half full' kind of person, always be the optimist, look for the sun after the rain.

One young woman whom I met at group sessions always dressed in black. As we opened up as a group, she shared with us why this was so. She felt that she was unattractive, even ugly. She thought her conversation dull and couldn't imagine anyone would choose to be her friend. Consequently she always wore black so as not to draw attention to herself. Dressed in black she felt she could disappear into anonymity and not be troubled by anyone. In fact, this lady was attractive, physically and as a person. As the weeks went by, she opened up, revealing intelligent conversation and a witty sense of humour. Towards the end of our sessions together, she arrived in a white t-shirt (under her black cardigan.) and was rewarded with a round of applause.

You are a valuable person. You are worthy of love and respect, from others and from yourself. Continue this journey with confidence and self-belief. If I could give you a bottle of motivation with this book, I would. That's not possible, so you must find out what motivates you and use it, whether it's family or friends, sports, cooking or even cleaning. My hope for you is that you begin and continue this journey and enjoy a happy and fulfilled life.

Organizations and Help Lines

United Kingdom

Victim support
Help line, 0845 30 30 90
www.victimsupport.org.uk

NAPAC (The national association for people abused in childhood.)
Freephone support line, 0800 085 3330
www.napac.org.uk

Support Line
Help line, 01708 765200
www.sexualabusesupport.org.uk

HAVOCA (Help for adult victims of child abuse.)
www.havoca.org.uk

Adult sexual abuse survivors support and information
www.aest.org.uk/

Survivors UK (Men)
Help line, 0845 122 1201
www.survivorsuk.org

Winchester rape and sexual abuse counselling
Help line, 01962 848024
Or   01962 848027
www.rasc.org.uk

Barnardo's
www.barnados.org.uk

Kingdom abuse survivors project (Fife)
01592 646644   leave a message and a counsellor will call back.
www.kasp.org.uk

Samaritans
Helpline, 08457 909090

United States of America

Adult survivor support groups
www.darkness2light.org

ASCA (adult survivors of child abuse)
The Morris Center
PO Box 14477
San Francisco
CA 94114
www.ascasupport.org

Adult victims of childhood abuse
www.fcasv.org

Recovering from childhood sexual abuse
www.wps.colostate.edu

Lightning Source UK Ltd.
Milton Keynes UK
UKOW021912281211

184477UK00012B/5/P